Abraham Lincoln

ABRAHAM LINCOLN GREW UP ON THE CRUDE, BRAWLING AMERICAN FRONTIER. HE FOUGHT, WRESTLED AND SWUNG AN AXE AS WELL AS ANY MAN. HE WENT TO SCHOOL LESS THAN A YEAR IN ALL HIS LIFE.

YET THE HOMELY, GAWKY, UNSCHOOLED BOY OF THE LOG CABIN GREW UP TO BE PRESIDENT OF THE UNITED STATES. AS PRESIDENT HE SAVED THE UNION FROM DESTRUCTION DURING THE BLOODY, TRAGIC YEARS OF THE AMERICAN CIVIL WAR.

BOY AND MAN, RAIL-SPLITTER AND PRESIDENT, ABRAHAM LINCOLN WAS WISE, STRONG, HUMOROUS, HUMBLE AND KIND. ALL OF HIS LIFE PEOPLE LOVED HIM BECAUSE HE WAS SO TRULY ONE OF THEM.

ABRAHAM LINCOLN WAS BORN ON FEBRUARY 12TH, 1809, IN A LOG CABIN ON NOLIN CREEK IN HARDIN COUNTY, KENTUCKY. HE WAS THE SON OF THOMAS AND NANCY HANKS LINCOLN.

WHAT SHALL WE NAME THE BOY, TOM?

I RECKON WE'LL CALL HIM ABRAHAM, AFTER HIS GRANDPAPPY WHO WAS KILLED BY THE INDIANS.

FROM THE TIME HE COULD WALK, ABE HAD TO HELP HIS FATHER IN THE FIELDS.

IF WE GET ALL THIS CORN PLANTED TODAY, I'LL LET YOU AND SARAH GO TO SCHOOL TOMORROW.

I'D LIKE TO GO, PAPPY. TEACHER SAID HE'D SHOW ME HOW TO WRITE MY WHOLE NAME NEXT TIME I CAME.

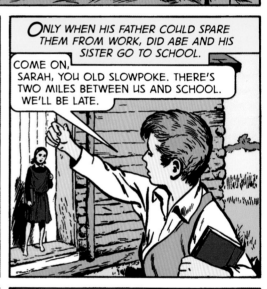

ONLY WHEN HIS FATHER COULD SPARE THEM FROM WORK, DID ABE AND HIS SISTER GO TO SCHOOL.

COME ON, SARAH, YOU OLD SLOWPOKE. THERE'S TWO MILES BETWEEN US AND SCHOOL. WE'LL BE LATE.

SOMETIMES ABE GOT TO GO FISHING, BUT HE DIDN'T ALWAYS KEEP THE FISH. ONE DAY...

HOWDY. ARE YOU A SOLDIER?

YOU BET I AM, SONNY. I'M JUST BACK FROM FIGHTING WITH ANDY JACKSON AT NEW ORLEANS.

YOU MUST BE HUNGRY AFTER COMING SO FAR. WON'T YOU TAKE MY FISH?

WELL, THANK YOU, BOY. I MUCH APPRECIATE IT.

WHEN ABE WAS SEVEN, THE LINCOLNS MOVED WEST TO THE INDIANA WILDERNESS. AT FIRST THEY LIVED IN A THREE-SIDED CABIN.

KEEP THE FIRE GOING, ABE. THAT'S ALL THAT STANDS BETWEEN US AND WINTER.

ABE HELPED HIS FATHER CUT DOWN TREES TO BUILD A REGULAR CABIN.

YOU DO A GOOD JOB, BOY. AT THE SPEED YOU'RE GROWING, YOU'LL SOON BE ABLE TO SPLIT THESE LOGS INTO RAILS.

TOM LINCOLN HUNTED GAME FOR THE FAMILY'S FOOD. ONE DAY...

HERE COMES A WHOLE FLOCK OF WILD TURKEYS. I WONDER IF I CAN GET ONE THE WAY PAPPY DOES.

USING HIS FATHER'S RIFLE, HE FIRED.

ABE BROUGHT DOWN A TURKEY, BUT HE WASN'T HAPPY ABOUT IT.

I RECKON I DON'T ENJOY KILLING A LIVING THING. I AIM TO AVOID IT AFTER THIS.

WHEN ABE WAS NINE HIS MOTHER DIED. THE NEXT YEAR HIS FATHER WENT TO KENTUCKY AND RETURNED WITH A WIFE.

COME AND MEET YOUR NEW MAMMY AND YOUR NEW SISTERS AND BROTHER.

HOWDY, ABE.

ABE'S STEPMOTHER, SARAH LINCOLN, ENCOURAGED HIM TO GO TO SCHOOL. AT NIGHT, HE PRACTICED WRITING AND ARITHMETIC.

LOOKS LIKE I'VE SQUEEZED IN AS MANY FIGURES AS THE SHOVEL WILL TAKE. IT'S TIME TO SHAVE THEM OFF AGAIN.

HE WENT TO SCHOOL LESS THAN A YEAR, BUT HE EDUCATED HIMSELF BY READING EVERY BOOK HE COULD FIND. ONE AFTERNOON...

DON'T TELL ME YOU WALKED TWENTY MILES JUST TO BORROW A BOOK FROM ME?

YES, SIR, I DID. YOU SEE THE THINGS I WANT TO KNOW ARE IN BOOKS. MY BEST FRIEND IS THE MAN WHO'LL GET ME ONE I HAVEN'T READ.

MOST OF THE TIME, THOUGH, ABE HAD TO WORK.

YOU KNOW, ABE, EVERYBODY THINKS YOU'RE A MITE LAZY WITH ALL YOUR READING. BUT YOU CAN WORK STEADY WHEN YOU'VE A MIND TO.

THAT'S BECAUSE MY PAPPY TAUGHT ME TO WORK HARD. BUT HE SURE NEVER TAUGHT ME TO LOVE IT.

ABE WAS FULL OF JOKES AND FUN. ONE DAY, WHEN HE WAS SEVENTEEN...

I CALCULATE YOU'RE A MITE SHY OF SIX FEET FOUR INCHES TALL. WATCH YOU KEEP YOUR HEAD CLEAN SO IT WON'T GO TRACKING UP MY CEILING.

YES, M'AM.

LATER, SARAH LINCOLN LEFT. ABE TOOK SOME NEIGHBOURHOOD BOYS ASIDE.

WHEN YOU GET YOUR FEET PLENTY MUDDY, I'LL HAVE SOME WORK FOR YOU TO DO.

HE HELPED EACH BOY WALK ACROSS THE CEILING OF THE CABIN.

STEP HARD, NOW.

WHEN SARAH LINCOLN RETURNED...

I DO DECLARE, YOU ARE THE LIMIT! IF YOU WEREN'T SO BIG, I'D SPANK YOU.

DON'T FRET, MAMMY. I AIM TO CLEAN IT UP AS SOON AS YOU'RE DONE LAUGHING.

THE NEIGHBOURS LOVED ABE FOR HIS HUMOUR AND FUNNY STORIES.

LAND'S SAKES, ABE! HOW YOU DO CARRY ON! WHATEVER WILL BECOME OF YOU?

OF ME M'AM? WHY, I'M GOING TO BE PRESIDENT OF THE UNITED STATES!

WHEN ABE WAS TWENTY-ONE, HIS FAMILY MOVED WEST AGAIN. EARLY ONE MORNING, THEY CROSSED THE SANGAMON RIVER IN ILLINOIS.

TARNATION! WE LEFT ONE OF THE DOGS ON THE OTHER SIDE. I RECKON HE'LL HAVE TO STAY THERE.

IT WOULDN'T BE KINDNESS TO LEAVE HIM, PAPPY.

ABE PLUNGED INTO THE ICY WATER AND BROUGHT THE DOG ACROSS.

THERE NOW, FELLOW. WE WOULDN'T LEAVE YOU BEHIND.

NEAR DECATUR, ILLINOIS, ABE HELPED HIS FAMILY BUILD A CABIN.

YOU SPLIT RAILS AS WELL AS ANY GROWN MAN.

I RECKON I AM A GROWN MAN, MAMMY.

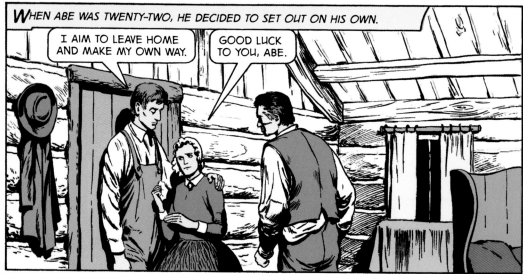

WHEN ABE WAS TWENTY-TWO, HE DECIDED TO SET OUT ON HIS OWN.

I AIM TO LEAVE HOME AND MAKE MY OWN WAY.

GOOD LUCK TO YOU, ABE.

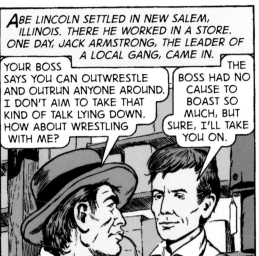

ABE LINCOLN SETTLED IN NEW SALEM, ILLINOIS. THERE HE WORKED IN A STORE. ONE DAY, JACK ARMSTRONG, THE LEADER OF A LOCAL GANG, CAME IN.

YOUR BOSS SAYS YOU CAN OUTWRESTLE AND OUTRUN ANYONE AROUND. I DON'T AIM TO TAKE THAT KIND OF TALK LYING DOWN. HOW ABOUT WRESTLING WITH ME?

THE BOSS HAD NO CAUSE TO BOAST SO MUCH, BUT SURE, I'LL TAKE YOU ON.

ALL THE MEN OF NEW SALEM TURNED OUT TO WATCH THE FIGHT.

LEM, I'LL BET YOU MY BEST SKINNING KNIFE THAT BOY LINCOLN'LL DOWN ARMSTRONG.

I'LL TAKE YOU UP ON THAT, SI.

THE TWO MEN WRESTLED HARD. FINALLY...

BUT ARMSTRONG'S FRIENDS WEREN'T GOING TO LET HIM BE BEATEN.

HEY, YOU CAN'T GET AWAY WITH THAT!

LINCOLN MOVED AWAY BEFORE THEY COULD GET HIM DOWN.

NOW THEN, FELLOWS, I'LL TAKE YOU ON, ONE BY ONE OR ALL TOGETHER. BUT I PREFER TO DO IT ON MY FEET.

NO ONE'S GOING TO TAKE YOU ON. YOU BEAT ME FAIR AND SQUARE. LET'S SHAKE AND BE FRIENDS.

THAT SUITS ME FINE.

IN NEW SALEM, LINCOLN BECAME FAMOUS FOR HIS HONESTY. ONE EVENING...

HOWDY M'AM. I ACCIDENTALLY CHARGED YOU SIX AND A QUARTER CENTS TOO MUCH TODAY. HERE IT IS.

LAND'S SAKES, MR LINCOLN! YOU ARE AS HONEST A MAN AS I'VE HEARD TELL OF. TO THINK YOU WALKED SIX MILES TO BRING ME A FEW PENNIES!

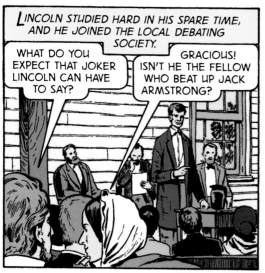

LINCOLN STUDIED HARD IN HIS SPARE TIME, AND HE JOINED THE LOCAL DEBATING SOCIETY.

WHAT DO YOU EXPECT THAT JOKER LINCOLN CAN HAVE TO SAY?

GRACIOUS! ISN'T HE THE FELLOW WHO BEAT UP JACK ARMSTRONG?

BUT LINCOLN SPOKE WELL AND IMPRESSED THE PEOPLE OF NEW SALEM.

THERE'S CERTAINLY MORE THAN JOKES IN YOUNG LINCOLN'S HEAD. HE MIGHT DO WELL AT POLITICS.

LINCOLN WAS ALREADY THINKING ABOUT GOING INTO POLITICS.

I RECKON POLITICS AND THE LAW ARE THE BEST WAYS TO GET AHEAD ON THE FRONTIER.

*H*E DECIDED TO RUN FOR THE STATE LEGISLATURE. BUT BEFORE HE COULD...

THE INDIAN CHIEF, BLACK HAWK, IS ON THE WARPATH. THE GOVERNOR'S CALLING FOR VOLUNTEERS TO FIGHT HIM.

I RECKON I'LL JOIN UP. HOW ABOUT YOU, JACK?

*J*ACK ARMSTRONG AND OTHER NEW SALEM MEN FORMED A COMPANY. THEY ELECTED LINCOLN THEIR CAPTAIN.

YOU DO ME MIGHTY PROUD, BOYS. I'LL DO MY BEST TO KEEP YOU HOPPING.

*L*INCOLN SAW NO ACTION, BUT HE EARNED THE RESPECT OF HIS MEN. ONE DAY, AN OLD INDIAN ARRIVED IN CAMP, THE MEN THREATENED TO KILL HIM.

DON'T HURT ME. I HAVE A PASS FROM THE GENERAL.

WHO CARES? THE ONLY GOOD INDIAN IS A DEAD ONE!

*L*INCOLN SAVED THE INDIAN'S LIFE.

HOLD ON, MEN. ANYONE WHO LAYS A HAND ON THIS OLD FELLOW WILL HAVE TO DEAL WITH ME.

AFTER HIS ENLISTMENT WAS OVER, LINCOLN RETURNED TO NEW SALEM AND CAMPAIGNED FOR THE STATE LEGISLATURE ON THE WHIG TICKET.

CAN'T THE PARTY DO ANY BETTER THAN THAT SCARECROW?

WAIT TILL YOU HEAR HIM. HE'S GOT SENSE FOR ALL HIS HOMELINESS.

I AM HUMBLE ABRAHAM LINCOLN. MY POLITICS ARE SHORT AND SWEET, LIKE THE OLD WOMAN'S DANCE. I AM IN FAVOUR OF A NATIONAL BANK AND INTERNAL IMPROVEMENTS. IF ELECTED I SHALL BE THANKFUL. IF NOT, IT WILL BE ALL THE SAME.

WHEN HE TRAVELLED TO NEARBY FARMS TO CAMPAIGN, HE TOOK PART IN WRESTLING MATCHES AND WORKED IN THE FIELDS.

I RECKON YOU'D LIKE FOR ME TO HELP YOU WITH THE HAY BEFORE YOU SETTLE DOWN TO LISTEN TO ME TALK.

ONCE, WHEN A FIGHT BROKE OUT AS HE WAS SPEAKING, HE THREW OUT THE MAN WHO HAD STARTED IT.

SORRY FOR THE INTERRUPTION, FOLKS. THIS'LL JUST TAKE A MINUTE.

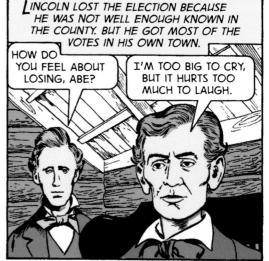

LINCOLN LOST THE ELECTION BECAUSE HE WAS NOT WELL ENOUGH KNOWN IN THE COUNTY. BUT HE GOT MOST OF THE VOTES IN HIS OWN TOWN.

HOW DO YOU FEEL ABOUT LOSING, ABE?

I'M TOO BIG TO CRY, BUT IT HURTS TOO MUCH TO LAUGH.

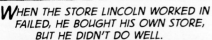

WHEN THE STORE LINCOLN WORKED IN FAILED, HE BOUGHT HIS OWN STORE, BUT HE DIDN'T DO WELL.

CAN I TROUBLE YOU FOR SOME CALICO*?

YES INDEED M'AM. I GUESS I WAS SO DEEP IN THIS BOOK I DIDN'T HEAR YOU COME IN.

*CLOTH

HE OFTEN TOOK TIME FROM WORK TO DO KINDNESSES FOR OTHERS.

HOWDY, AB. WHAT ARE YOU UP TO?

CHOPPING WOOD TO EARN A DOLLAR TO BUY ME SOME SHOES, MR LINCOLN.

IT'S MIGHTY COLD FOR THAT. NOW YOU GO ON INTO MY STORE AND WARM YOUR FEET IN FRONT OF THE STOVE. I'LL BE ALONG IN A BIT.

AN HOUR LATER...

HERE'S YOUR AXE, AB. THE WOOD'S ALL CHOPPED. YOU GO COLLECT YOUR DOLLAR AND BUY THOSE SHOES.

BY CRACKY, MR LINCOLN, YOU'RE A PRINCE!

LINCOLN'S STORE FAILED. THEN HE GOT A JOB AS POSTMASTER OF NEW SALEM.

GOOD DAY, M'AM. I'VE GOT SOMETHING IN MY HAT FOR YOU.

LINCOLN WAS CARELESS ABOUT HIS OWN MONEY, BUT HE WAS VERY CAREFUL ABOUT THE GOVERNMENT'S.

HAVE YOU THE POST OFFICE MONEY FOR ME, MR LINCOLN?

I'VE GOT IT HERE TO THE PENNY.

LINCOLN ALSO HELD MANY OTHER JOBS. ONE DAY...

I DO DECLARE, ABE, YOU'RE AS LAZY AS AN OLD HOUND DOG. READING INSTEAD OF WORKING IS MORE THAN I CAN CREDIT.

BUT I'M NOT READING. I'M STUDYING LAW.

LAW? WHAT ARE YOU DOING THAT FOR?

BACK IN INDIANA, WHEN I WAS A BOY, I USED TO HANG AROUND THE COURTHOUSE. EVER SINCE, I'VE HANKERED TO TALK FANCY AND MOVE PEOPLE THE WAY LAWYERS DO.

IN 1834 LINCOLN AGAIN RAN FOR THE STATE LEGISLATURE. THIS TIME HE WON. BEFORE HIS TERM BEGAN, HE BORROWED SOME MONEY.

I NEED IT TO BUY A SUIT OF CLOTHES. WHEN THOSE FANCY POLITICIANS SEE ME, I DON'T WANT THEM TO JUDGE MY KERNEL BY MY SHELL.

LINCOLN SERVED FOUR TERMS IN THE LEGISLATURE. HE LEARNED HOW TO GET ALONG WITH POLITICIANS. HE ALSO LEARNED THAT THERE WERE SOME ISSUES ON WHICH HE COULD NOT COMPROMISE.

I BELIEVE THAT SLAVERY IS BOTH UNJUST AND BAD POLICY. I CANNOT SUPPORT IT.

IN 1836 LINCOLN PASSED HIS BAR EXAMINATION. THE FOLLOWING YEAR, HE MOVED TO SPRINGFIELD, ILLINOIS. HE BECAME JOHN STUART'S LAW PARTNER.

WELCOME TO THE OFFICE. YOU'LL BE MIGHTY BUSY IN IT, FOR I'LL BE AWAY MOST OF THE TIME RUNNING FOR CONGRESS.

IT WON'T HURT ME AT ALL TO STAY HERE AND RUN FOR JUSTICE.

LINCOLN PRACTICED LAW IN SPRINGFIELD AND NEARBY TOWNS. WHEN HE RODE FROM ONE PLACE TO ANOTHER, HE READ BOOKS - ANYTHING FROM JOKE BOOKS TO CLASSICS.

LINCOLN NEVER TOOK A CASE HE DIDN'T BELIEVE IN.

YOU'LL HAVE TO GET ANOTHER LAWYER. I CAN'T DO IT. WHILE I'D BE TALKING TO THE JURY, I'D BE THINKING, "LINCOLN, YOU'RE A LIAR." I BELIEVE I MIGHT FORGET MYSELF AND SAY IT ALOUD.

HIS OFFICE HAD A TRAPDOOR INTO THE COUNTY COURTROOM BELOW. ONE DAY SOME WHIGS USED THE COURTROOM FOR CAMPAIGN SPEECHES.

A DEMOCRATIC NEWSPAPER WILL ALWAYS DEFEND CORRUPTION.

THAT'S A LIE! PULL HIM DOWN! PULL HIM DOWN!

ABOVE, IN HIS OFFICE, LINCOLN SAW THE FIGHT BEGIN.

HE QUICKLY SWUNG DOWN INTO THE COURTROOM.

HOLD ON, GENTLEMEN. THIS MAN HAS A RIGHT TO SPEAK. IF YOU ATTACK HIM, YOU'LL HAVE TO TAKE ME ON, TOO.

AS A RISING LAWYER AND LEGISLATOR, LINCOLN TOOK PART IN SPRINGFIELD'S SOCIAL LIFE. AT A BALL IN 1840 HE MET MARY TODD.

TELL ME, BILLY, WHO'S THAT PRETTY GAL OVER THERE?

THAT'S THE SISTER OF THE GOVERNOR'S DAUGHTER-IN-LAW. SHE'S UP FROM KENTUCKY.

LINCOLN AND MARY TODD WERE INTRODUCED.

MISS TODD, I WANT TO DANCE WITH YOU IN THE WORST WAY.

AND THAT WAS THE WAY HE DANCED.

LATER...

I SAW YOU WITH THAT GREAT GAWK, MR LINCOLN. I HEAR HE'S VERY BRIGHT, BUT HE'S CERTAINLY OUT OF PLACE IN A DRAWING ROOM.

I LIKE HIM, THOUGH. HE'S VERY KIND AND SINCERE.

LINCOLN ALSO LIKED MARY TODD. ON NOVEMBER 4TH, 1842, THEY WERE MARRIED.

THE NEXT YEAR THE LINCOLNS HAD THEIR FIRST SON, ROBERT. A SECOND SON, EDWARD, WAS BORN IN 1846, THE YEAR LINCOLN RAN FOR CONGRESS.

WELL, MOTHER, I MAY SOON BE GOING TO WASHINGTON, IF I CAN BEAT THAT OLD FIRE-EATER, CARTWRIGHT.

HIS OPPONENT WAS PETER CARTWRIGHT, A FIREY PREACHER. ONE NIGHT, LINCOLN ATTENDED A MEETING WHERE CARTWRIGHT WAS SPEAKING.

ALL WHO DO NOT WISH TO GO TO HELL WILL STAND.

EVERYONE STOOD BUT LINCOLN.

MAY I INQUIRE, MR LINCOLN JUST WHERE YOU ARE GOING?

IF IT IS ALL THE SAME TO YOU, I AM GOING TO CONGRESS.

LINCOLN WON THE ELECTION AND WENT TO WASHINGTON. HE LEARNED ABOUT THE GOVERNMENT, BUT HE SAW THINGS THAT MADE HIM UNHAPPY.

IT IS A DISGRACE FOR SLAVERY TO BE ALLOWED HERE, IN THE CAPITAL OF THE UNITED STATES!

WHEN HE WAS NOT IN CONGRESS, LINCOLN OFTEN WENT BOWLING.

DID I EVER TELL YOU HOW BACK WHEN I WAS A POSTMASTER, A FELLOW CAME ASKING IF I HAD ANY MAIL FOR HIM? I DIDN'T RECOLLECT HIS NAME SO I ASKED HIM WHAT IT WAS.

DO YOU KNOW WHAT THE SMART ALEC SAID TO ME? HE SAID, "YOU'LL FIND MY NAME ON THE ENVELOPE, BY GUM!"

AFTER HIS TERM ENDED, IN 1849, LINCOLN RETURNED TO SPRINGFIELD.

I'VE HAD ENOUGH POLITICS FOR A WHILE, MOTHER. I THINK I'LL STICK TO THE LAW AND HAVE MORE TIME FOR THESE RASCALS.

LINCOLN ADORED HIS SONS. HE LIKED TO TAKE THEM FOR A RIDE IN THEIR WAGON.

HE DIDN'T NOTICE WHEN EDDIE FELL OUT ONE DAY.

EXCUSE ME, MR LINCOLN, BUT YOU'VE LOST ONE OF YOUR BOYS.

BLESS MY SOUL, SO I HAVE! I WAS THINKING SO HARD I PLUMB FORGOT WHAT I WAS DOING.

IN 1850 EDDIE DIED. A FEW MONTHS LATER, ANOTHER SON, WILLIAM, WAS BORN.

WELL, MOTHER, I RECKON THAT LITTLE WILLIE WILL HELP EASE OUR LOSS.

THREE YEARS LATER, THE LINCOLNS HAD THEIR FOURTH AND LAST SON, THOMAS.

LOOK AT YOUR LITTLE BROTHER. HE'S AS SQUIRMY AS A TADPOLE. AND THAT'S WHAT WE'LL CALL HIM – TAD FOR TADPOLE.

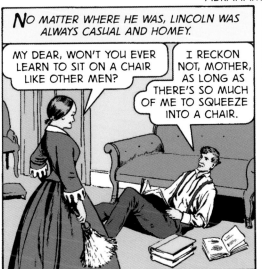

NO MATTER WHERE HE WAS, LINCOLN WAS ALWAYS CASUAL AND HOMEY.

MY DEAR, WON'T YOU EVER LEARN TO SIT ON A CHAIR LIKE OTHER MEN?

I RECKON NOT, MOTHER, AS LONG AS THERE'S SO MUCH OF ME TO SQUEEZE INTO A CHAIR.

ONE DAY...

GOOD MORNING. IS MRS LINCOLN HOME?

JUST A MINUTE, LADIES, WHILE I LOOK OVER THE HOUSE.

HE FOUND THAT HIS WIFE WAS STILL DRESSING.

SHE'LL BE DOWN AS SOON AS SHE GETS HER TROTTING HARNESS ON.

ONCE THE LOCAL VOLUNTEER FIREMEN ASKED LINCOLN FOR A CONTRIBUTION.

WELL NOW, BOYS, I'D LIKE TO GIVE YOU TWENTY-FIVE DOLLARS. BUT FIRST I'LL HAVE TO TALK IT OVER AT HOME.

LINCOLN TOLD HIS WIFE ABOUT THE REQUEST.

I THOUGHT IT'D BE RIGHT GENEROUS TO GIVE THEM FIFTY DOLLARS.

FIFTY DOLLARS! YOU'D THINK MONEY GREW ON TREES! TWENTY-FIVE IS QUITE ENOUGH!

AND THE NEXT MORNING...

HERE'S YOUR MONEY, BOYS. MRS LINCOLN AND I AGREED ON TWENTY-FIVE DOLLARS.

LINCOLN'S KINDNESS KEPT HIM FROM MAKING MUCH MONEY. ONCE A MAN ASKED HIS LAWYER TO HAVE LINCOLN HELP DEFEND HIM.

HERE'S TEN DOLLARS TO PAY YOU BOTH. IT'S ALL THE MONEY I HAVE.

WHAT ABOUT YOUR WIFE? WON'T SHE NEED THIS?

SHE'LL MAKE OUT SOMEHOW.

SOMEHOW IS NOT ENOUGH. I'LL GIVE HER FIVE DOLLARS. YOUR LAWYER AND I WILL DIVIDE THE REST.

BY PRACTICING LAW ALL OVER THE STATE, HE GOT TO KNOW PEOPLE AND RESPECT THEM.

YOU CAN FOOL SOME OF THE PEOPLE ALL THE TIME, AND ALL THE PEOPLE SOME OF THE TIME, BUT YOU CAN'T FOOL ALL THE PEOPLE ALL THE TIME.

HE READ EVERY NEWSPAPER HE COULD FIND IN ORDER TO KNOW AS MUCH AS POSSIBLE ABOUT WHAT WAS HAPPENING. HE SOMETIMES ANNOYED HIS NEW LAW PARTNER, WILLIAM HERNDON.

DO YOU ALWAYS HAVE TO READ ALOUD, MR LINCOLN?

I RECKON I DO, BILLY. IT SEEMS TO ME IT BRINGS TWO SENSES TO BEAR ON THE NEWS AT ONCE – MY EYES AND MY EARS.

THE NEWS WAS FILLED WITH THE GROWING BITTERNESS BETWEEN THE NORTH AND THE SOUTH OVER SLAVERY. LINCOLN THOUGHT THE PROBLEM THROUGH.

ALTHOUGH VOLUME UPON VOLUME IS WRITTEN TO PROVE SLAVERY A GOOD THING, WE NEVER HEAR OF THE MAN WHO WISHES TO TAKE THE GOOD OF IT BY BEING A SLAVE HIMSELF.

IN 1854 LINCOLN RAN FOR THE ILLINOIS LEGISLATURE AND WON. THEN HE RAN FOR SENATOR FROM ILLINOIS AND LOST.

WELL, MOTHER, IT SEEMS AS THOUGH I WON'T GET TO WASHINGTON THIS YEAR.

ALL OVER AMERICA, SLAVERY WAS BECOMING A MAJOR ISSUE. IN KANSAS, CIVIL WAR THREATENED OVER WHETHER IT WOULD BE A SLAVE OR A FREE STATE.

CAN WE AS A NATION CONTINUE TOGETHER PERMANENTLY HALF SLAVE AND HALF FREE?

IN MAY, 1856, IN ILLINOIS, THE WHIGS AND OTHER PARTIES JOINED TO BECOME THE ANTI-SLAVERY REPUBLICAN PARTY. LINCOLN WAS ASKED TO SPEAK TO THE ILLINOIS REPUBLICAN CONVENTION.

SAY, HE'S GREAT! I'M GOING TO LISTEN INSTEAD OF TAKING NOTES. MY NEWSPAPER CAN USE SOMEONE ELSE'S STORY.

BUT NO ONE TOOK NOTES. THERE IS NO RECORD OF WHAT MAY HAVE BEEN LINCOLN'S GREATEST SPEECH BECAUSE PEOPE WERE TOO EXCITED TO WRITE DOWN WHAT THEY HEARD!

ILLINOIS POLITICIANS WERE IMPRESSED.

THAT'S THE GREATEST SPEECH EVER MADE HERE. IT HIT TO THE HEART OF THE SLAVERY QUESTION.

BY 1858 LINCOLN WAS A DISTINGUISHED LAWYER AND POLITICIAN. BUT WHEN HE HEARD THAT THE SON OF HIS OLD FRIEND, JACK ARMSTRONG WAS ACCUSED OF MURDER, HE DROPPED ALL HIS WORK AND HURRIED TO ARMSTRONG'S WIDOW.

IT'S KIND OF YOU TO OFFER TO HELP DEFEND DUFF, BUT I HAVE NO MONEY FOR EXPENSIVE LAWYERS.

YOU NEED NONE, AUNT HANNAH. WE GO TO TRIAL TODAY. I'LL HAVE DUFF FREE BEFORE SUNDOWN.

LINCOLN CROSS-EXAMINED THE PRINCIPAL WITNESS AGAINST DUFF ARMSTRONG.

HOW WAS IT YOU COULD SEE THE DEFENDANT STRIKE THE VICTIM IF THE MURDER TOOK PLACE BETWEEN TEN AND ELEVEN AT NIGHT?

EASY. BY THE LIGHT OF THE MOON WHICH WAS SHINING JUST ABOUT STRAIGHT OVERHEAD.

ACCORDING TO THIS ALMANAC, ON THAT NIGHT, THE MOON HAD SET BY 11:57. I ASK YOU: WOULDN'T THAT MEAN THAT AT ELEVEN THE MOON WAS TOO LOW IN THE SKY FOR ANYONE TO SEE ANYTHING?

LINCOLN SPOKE MOVINGLY TO THE JURY.

I HAVE KNOWN THIS BOY'S FAMILY TWENTY-SIX YEARS. I HAVE ROCKED HIM IN HIS CRADLE. HE MAY BE WILD, BUT HE IS NOT A MURDERER. I DON'T NEED THE ALMANAC TO TELL ME SO.

LATER THAT DAY, THE JURY CAME IN WITH ITS VERDICT.

NOT GUILTY.

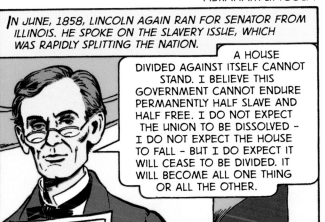

IN JUNE, 1858, LINCOLN AGAIN RAN FOR SENATOR FROM ILLINOIS. HE SPOKE ON THE SLAVERY ISSUE, WHICH WAS RAPIDLY SPLITTING THE NATION.

A HOUSE DIVIDED AGAINST ITSELF CANNOT STAND. I BELIEVE THIS GOVERNMENT CANNOT ENDURE PERMANENTLY HALF SLAVE AND HALF FREE. I DO NOT EXPECT THE UNION TO BE DISSOLVED – I DO NOT EXPECT THE HOUSE TO FALL – BUT I DO EXPECT IT WILL CEASE TO BE DIVIDED. IT WILL BECOME ALL ONE THING OR ALL THE OTHER.

LINCOLN CHALLENGED HIS OPPONENT, STEPHEN DOUGLAS, TO A SERIES OF SEVEN DEBATES ON SLAVERY. DOUGLAS TRIED TO TURN LINCOLN'S "HOUSE DIVIDED" SPEECH AGAINST HIM.

LINCOLN WANTS WAR BETWEEN THE STATES.

LINCOLN DENIED THIS.

NO ONE WANTS WAR LESS THAN I. BUT THE UNION IS FAST APPROACHING A CRISIS. IT MUST DECIDE WHICH WAY TO GO ON SLAVERY.

DOUGLAS TRAVELLED TO THE DEBATES IN HIS PRIVATE RAILROAD CAR. LINCOLN WAS OFTEN A PASSENGER ON THE SAME TRAIN.

THE LINCOLN-DOUGLAS DEBATES MADE LINCOLN A NATIONAL FIGURE, EVEN THOUGH HE LOST THE ELECTION.

HOW DO YOU FEEL ABOUT LOSING?

I RECKON I LOOK ON IT AS ONLY A SLIP AND NOT A FALL, BILLY.

TWO YEARS LATER LINCOLN WAS ASKED TO SPEAK ON SLAVERY AT COOPER UNION IN NEW YORK.

WRONG AS WE THINK SLAVERY IS, WE CAN YET AFFORD TO LET IT ALONE WHERE IT IS. BUT CAN WE ALLOW IT TO SPREAD AND OVERRUN US HERE IN THE FREE STATES?

AFTER THIS SPEECH, PEOPLE BEGAN TO TALK OF LINCOLN RUNNING FOR PRESIDENT. IN MAY, 1860, ILLINOIS REPUBLICANS NOMINATED HIM AS THEIR CANDIDATE.

DID YOU SPLIT THESE RAILS?

MAYBE I DID AND MAYBE I DIDN'T. I CAN SAY, THOUGH, THAT I HAVE SPLIT A GOOD MANY BETTER ONES.

A WEEK LATER, THE NATIONAL REPUBLICAN CONVENTION MET IN CHICAGO AND NOMINATED ABRAHAM LINCOLN FOR PRESIDENT. HE WAS IN THE SPRINGFIELD TELEGRAPH OFFICE WHEN THE NEWS CAME.

IF YOU WILL EXCUSE ME, THERE IS A LITTLE SHORT WOMAN AT OUR HOUSE WHO IS PROBABLY MORE INTERESTED IN THIS DISPATCH THAN I AM.

THE PRESIDENTIAL ELECTION OF 1860 CENTERED ON THE ISSUE OF SLAVERY. LINCOLN REFUSED TO MAKE CAMPAIGN SPEECHES.

THOSE WHO WILL NOT READ OR HEED WHAT I HAVE ALREADY PUBLICLY SAID, WOULD NOT READ, OR HEED, A REPETITION OF IT. AN HONEST MAN WILL FIND IN OUR PLATFORM ANYTHING I COULD SAY.

THE REPUBLICAN PARTY OPPOSED THE EXTENSION OF SLAVERY INTO NEW TERRITORIES. THE SOUTH FEARED THAT A REPUBLICAN VICTORY WOULD MEAN THE END OF SLAVERY.

CAN'T YOU SAY SOMETHING TO PACIFY THE HONEST MEN OF THE SOUTH?

NO. IF I APPEARED TO COMPROMISE WITH THEM, I WOULD GO TO WASHINGTON WITHOUT THE SUPPORT OF THE MEN WHO NOW SUPPORT ME. I WOULD BE AS POWERLESS AS A BLOCK OF WOOD.

LINCOLN RAN AGAINST THREE OTHER CANDIDATES. IN NOVEMBER, HE WAS ELECTED PRESIDENT OF THE UNITED STATES.

MARY, WE'RE ELECTED!

WITH LINCOLN'S VICTORY, THE SOUTH BEGAN TO SPEAK OF SECESSION.

THE NORTH MEANS TO FREE YOUR SLAVES. WHEN THAT IS DONE, NO PEN CAN DESCRIBE THE HORRORS THAT WILL OVERSPREAD THIS COUNTRY. DISUNION IS A FEARFUL THING, BUT EMANCIPATION IS WORSE!

ON DECEMBER 20TH, SOUTH CAROLINA SECEDED FROM THE UNION. BY FEBRUARY, 1861, SIX OTHER SOUTHERN STATES HAD JOINED IT AND FORMED THE CONFEDERATE STATES OF AMERICA.

WHILE WAITING TO TAKE OFFICE, LINCOLN CAREFULLY CHOSE MEN FOR HIS CABINET.

YOU ARE APPOINTING THE VERY REPUBLICANS WHO OPPOSED YOU.

BUT THEY ARE THE BEST MEN IN THE PARTY. WHEN A MAN BUILDS A HOUSE, HE USES THE BEST TIMBER AVAILABLE. I WANT THE SAME FOR MY CABINET.

HE ALSO BEGAN TO GROW A BEARD.

YOUR BEARD FEELS SO FUNNY, PA. WHY ARE YOU GROWING IT?

TWO REASONS, WILLIE. A LITTLE GIRL WROTE ME THAT I WOULD LOOK NICE WITH ONE. AND SOME OF MY FELLOW POLITICIANS HINTED THAT IT WOULD MAKE ME LOOK MORE DIGNIFIED.

LINCOLN SAID GOODBYE TO HIS LAW PARTNER, WILLIAM HERNDON, BEFORE LEAVING FOR WASHINGTON.

SHALL I TAKE YOUR NAME OFF THE SIGN?

NO, BILLY, LEAVE IT AS IT IS. IF I LIVE, I'M COMING BACK SOMETIME. THEN WE'LL GO ON PRACTICING LAW TOGETHER AS IF NOTHING HAD HAPPENED.

ON FEBRUARY 11TH, LINCOLN LEFT SPRINGFIELD. A CROWD WAS AT THE STATION.

MY FRIENDS, NO ONE, NOT IN MY SITUATION, CAN APPRECIATE MY FEELING OF SADNESS AT THIS PARTING. TO THIS PLACE, AND THE KINDNESS OF THESE PEOPLE, I OWE EVERYTHING. HERE I HAVE LIVED A QUARTER OF A CENTURY, AND HAVE PASSED FROM A YOUNG TO AN OLD MAN. HERE MY CHILDREN HAVE BEEN BORN, AND ONE IS BURIED.

I NOW LEAVE, NOT KNOWING WHEN, OR WHETHER EVER, I MAY RETURN. TRUSTING IN HIM, WHO CAN GO WITH ME, AND REMAIN WITH YOU, AND BE EVERYWHERE FOR GOOD, LET US CONFIDENTLY HOPE THAT ALL WILL YET BE WELL. TO HIS CARE COMMENDING YOU, AS I HOPE IN YOUR PRAYERS YOU WILL COMMEND ME, I BID YOU AN AFFECTIONATE FAREWELL.

ON THE WAY TO WASHINGTON, ALLAN PINKERTON, A PRIVATE DETECTIVE, WARNED LINCOLN OF A PLOT TO ASSASSINATE HIM.

BUT WHY SHOULD ANYONE WANT TO KILL ME?

YOU DO NOT REALISE HOW FANATICAL SOUTHERNERS ARE ABOUT YOUR ELECTION. SOME ARE DETERMINED YOU WILL NEVER GET TO WASHINGTON ALIVE.

HE ADVISED LINCOLN TO GO TO WASHINGTON SECRETLY. THE NEXT DAY LINCOLN AND A FRIEND, WARD HILL LAMON, SLIPPED OUT OF HARRISBURG, PENNSYLVANIA.

YOU'RE A REGULAR WALKING ARMY, HILL. I'VE NO DOUBT WE'LL GET SAFELY TO WASHINGTON.

WHEN THEY LEFT HARRISBURG ALL THE TELEGRAPH WIRES WERE CUT SO THE NEWS COULD NOT LEAK OUT. PINKERTON MET THEM IN PHILADELPHIA.

ONE OF MY WOMEN DETECTIVES HAS RESERVED BERTHS FOR HER "INVALID BROTHER" AND HIS COMPANION. THEY ARE FOR US.

THE NEXT MORNING, THEY ARRIVED IN WASHINGTON. A MAN APPROACHED THEM.

DON'T HIT HIM, HILL. HE'S NOT AN ASSASSIN. HE'S CONGRESSMAN WASHBURNE.

ON MARCH 4TH, LINCOLN WAS INAUGURATED THE SIXTEENTH PRESIDENT OF THE UNITED STATES. IN HIS SPEECH, HE SAID THAT SECESSION FROM THE UNION MEANT ANARCHY. HE PUT THE RESPONSIBILITY FOR CIVIL WAR ON THE SOUTH.

IN YOUR HANDS, MY DISSATISFIED FELLOW-COUNTRYMEN, AND NOT IN MINE IS THE MOMENTOUS ISSUE OF CIVIL WAR. YOU HAVE NO OATH REGISTERED IN HEAVEN TO DESTROY THE GOVERNMENT, WHILE I SHALL HAVE THE MOST SOLEMN ONE TO "PRESERVE, PROTECT AND DEFEND" IT.

Six weeks later, on April 12th, 1861, a Confederate battery fired on Federal Fort Sumter in Charleston Harbour, South Carolina. The Civil War had begun.

By June, four other Southern states had joined the Confederate States of America. Lincoln proclaimed a state of insurrection.

WE MUST SETTLE THIS QUESTION NOW, WHETHER IN A FREE GOVERNMENT THE MINORITY HAVE THE RIGHT TO BREAK UP THE GOVERNMENT WHENEVER THEY CHOOSE. IF WE FAIL IT WILL GO FAR TO PROVE THE INCAPABILITY OF THE PEOPLE TO GOVERN THEMSELVES.

He called for troops to suppress the rebellion and to defend Washington. Day after day he waited.

IF OUR TROOPS DON'T COME SOON, THE VIRGINIA HILLS OVER THERE WILL BE COVERED WITH REBELS. THEY'LL TAKE WASHINGTON AS EASY AS I'D SQUASH A MOSQUITO.

Finally Northern troops arrived.

"WE ARE COMING, FATHER ABRAHAM, THREE HUNDRED THOUSAND MORE."

IN JULY, 1861, PEOPLE DROVE GAILY OUT OF WASHINGTON TO WATCH THE FIRST BIG BATTLE OF THE WAR.

WELL, MY DEAR, IT WILL BE QUITE A LARK TO SEE THE NORTH WHIP THE SOUTH TODAY.

BUT IN THE FIERCE BATTLE AT MANASSAS, VIRGINIA, A CONFEDERATE ARMY BEAT THE UNION ARMY OF THE POTOMAC.

THE NEXT MORNING, THE PRESIDENT SADLY WATCHED THE DEFEATED ARMY RETURN.

THIS WILL BE NO EASY WAR, TO BE WON IN A SUMMER'S BATTLE. IT WILL BE A TERRIBLE ORDEAL.

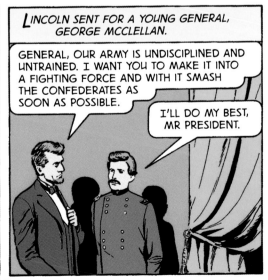

LINCOLN SENT FOR A YOUNG GENERAL, GEORGE MCCLELLAN.

GENERAL, OUR ARMY IS UNDISCIPLINED AND UNTRAINED. I WANT YOU TO MAKE IT INTO A FIGHTING FORCE AND WITH IT SMASH THE CONFEDERATES AS SOON AS POSSIBLE.

I'LL DO MY BEST, MR PRESIDENT.

THE MEN AND BOYS IN THE NORTHERN ARMY WERE TOTALLY UNUSED TO THE DISCIPLINE OF WAR. EVERY DAY LINCOLN HAD TO DECIDE WHETHER TO SENTENCE TO DEATH A SOLDIER WHO HAD DESERTED OR FALLEN ASLEEP ON DUTY. WHENEVER HE COULD, HE COMMUTED THE SENTENCE.

IT WOULD FRIGHTEN THE POOR FELLOWS TOO TERRIBLY TO KILL THEM. BESIDES, I DO NOT THINK AN HONEST, BRAVE SOLDIER, CONSCIOUS OF NO CRIME BUT SLEEPING WHEN HE WAS TIRED, OUGHT TO BE SHOT OR HANGED. THE COUNTRY HAS BETTER USES FOR HIM.

ONE DAY, A DELEGATION OF VERMONT SOLDIERS CAME TO SEE HIM.

WE'VE COME ABOUT OUR FRIEND, WILLIAM SCOTT, SIR. HE'S SLATED TO BE SHOT FOR SLEEPING ON SENTRY DUTY. HE'S NO COWARD. BUT HE'S NOT USED TO KEEPING AWAKE AT NIGHT.

I'LL SEE WHAT I CAN DO FOR HIM, BOYS.

IN THE PRESS OF WORK, LINCOLN FORGOT ABOUT SCOTT. AT THE LAST MINUTE, HE REMEMBERED.

HURRY! IT'S A MATTER OF LIFE AND DEATH!

HE REACHED THE TENT WHERE SCOTT WAS A PRISONER.

MY BOY, YOU WILL NOT BE SHOT TOMORROW. YOU MAY GO BACK TO YOUR REGIMENT.

MR PRESIDENT, WHAT CAN I DO TO REPAY YOU?

ONLY ONE MAN IN THE WORLD CAN PAY MY BILL. HIS NAME IS WILLIAM SCOTT. IF FROM THIS DAY YOU DO YOUR DUTY AS A SOLDIER, THEN MY DEBT WILL BE PAID. WILL YOU PROMISE?

I PROMISE, AND WITH GOD'S HELP I WILL KEEP THIS PROMISE.

SOMETIMES THE PRESIDENT HAD EASIER PARDONS TO GIVE. ONE DAY HIS SONS, WILLIE AND TAD, WERE PLAYING WITH FRIENDS.

YOU, JACK, ARE SENTENCED TO BE SHOT AT SUNRISE FOR SLEEPING ON PICKET DUTY.

THE HEAD GARDENER CAME BY.

IT SEEMS A PITY TO BURY HIM, BOYS. WHY DON'T YOU HAVE HIM PARDONED?

A FEW MINUTES LATER...

PA! PA! JACK WILL BE SHOT FOR SLEEPING ON GUARD DUTY UNLESS YOU PARDON HIM. WILL YOU?

YES, TAD. I BELIEVE THAT CAN BE ARRANGED.

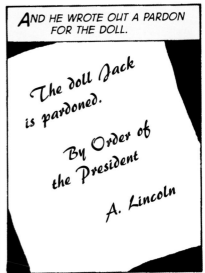

AND HE WROTE OUT A PARDON FOR THE DOLL.

The doll Jack is pardoned.

By Order of the President

A. Lincoln

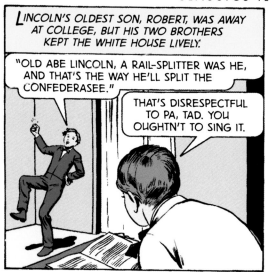

LINCOLN'S OLDEST SON, ROBERT, WAS AWAY AT COLLEGE, BUT HIS TWO BROTHERS KEPT THE WHITE HOUSE LIVELY.

"OLD ABE LINCOLN, A RAIL-SPLITTER WAS HE, AND THAT'S THE WAY HE'LL SPLIT THE CONFEDERASEE."

THAT'S DISRESPECTFUL TO PA, TAD. YOU OUGHTN'T TO SING IT.

I DON'T CARE, WILLIE. EVERYBODY KNOWS PA USED TO SPLIT RAILS.

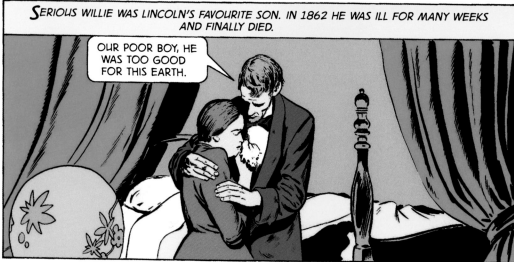

SERIOUS WILLIE WAS LINCOLN'S FAVOURITE SON. IN 1862 HE WAS ILL FOR MANY WEEKS AND FINALLY DIED.

OUR POOR BOY, HE WAS TOO GOOD FOR THIS EARTH.

LINCOLN WAS HEARTBROKEN. A FEW MONTHS LATER, A FIRE BROKE OUT IN THE WHITE HOUSE STABLES.

HAVE THE HORSES BEEN TAKEN OUT?

GUARDS MADE LINCOLN RETURN TO THE WHITE HOUSE.

I'M SORRY MR PRESIDENT, BUT THE FIRE MAY BE AN ASSASSIN'S TRICK TO LURE YOU OUT.

MAYBE SO. ALL I KNOW IS THAT WILLIE'S PONY IS IN THE STABLE. I WOULD HAVE LIKED TO HAVE SAVED IT FOR HIM.

YOUNG TAD LINCOLN MANAGED TO KEEP BUSY ALL BY HIMSELF. ONE DAY SOME VISITING LADIES HEARD AN AWFUL NOISE IN THE EAST ROOM OF THE WHITE HOUSE.

GOOD GRACIOUS! WHAT CAN THAT RACKET BE?

LOOK OUT THERE! MAKE WAY! MAKE WAY!

TAD BECAME HIS FATHER'S CLOSEST COMPANION. LINCOLN OFTEN READ TO HIM IN THE EVENING.

THE SECRETARY OF WAR GAVE TAD A COMMISSION.

I COMMISSION YOU, THOMAS LINCOLN, A LIEUTENANT IN THE UNITED STATES ARMY.

HE ORGANISED THE WHITE HOUSE SERVANTS INTO A GUARD.

I HAVE DISMISSED THE REGULAR GUARDS. TONIGHT YOU ARE ALL ON SENTRY DUTY IN THE WHITE HOUSE. DO YOU ALL UNDERSTAND WHAT YOU ARE TO DO?

YES, SIR.

LATER THAT EVENING...

MY COMPANY IS GUARDING THE WHITE HOUSE TONIGHT, MR PRESIDENT. ALL IS SAFE.

THANK YOU, LIEUTENANT TAD. I'M MOST RELIEVED TO HEAR THAT.

LINCOLN SPENT MUCH OF HIS TIME TRYING TO GET GENERAL MCCLELLAN TO FIGHT THE CONFEDERATE ARMY.

I WISH MCCLELLAN WOULD GO AT THE ENEMY. IF HE DOESN'T WANT TO USE THE ARMY, I'D LIKE TO BORROW IT.

MCCLELLAN ORGANISED THE UNION ARMY OF THE POTOMAC INTO A SUPERB FIGHTING FORCE. BUT MONTH AFTER MONTH, HE PUT OFF GOING INTO BATTLE.

WE CAN'T TAKE THE CONFEDERATE POSITION AT MANASSAS, VIRGINIA. MY SPIES TELL ME IT IS TOO STRONGLY FORTIFIED.

IN THE SPRING OF 1842 THE CONFEDERATES WITHDREW FROM MANASSAS. WHEN MCCLELLAN'S MEN EXAMINED THEIR FORTIFICATIONS...

WELL, I'LL BE A SON OF A GUN! ALL THOSE CANNON THEY'VE BEEN POINTING AT US WERE ONLY LOGS!

AFTER THIS, LINCOLN BEGAN TO DIRECT THE WAR HIMSELF. HE REALISED THAT A GREAT IDEAL WAS NEEDED TO UNITE THE COUNTRY IN THE WAR EFFORT.

GENTLEMEN, WE MUST DO MORE THAN SAVE THE UNION. WE MUST END THE HUMAN BONDAGE OF SLAVERY. I PROPOSE TO EMANCIPATE THE SLAVES.

AN EMANCIPATION PROCLAMATION WAS POSTPONED UNTIL AFTER A UNION VICTORY. FINALLY, IN SEPTEMBER, 1862, THE UNION ARMY STOPPED CONFEDERATE GENERAL ROBERT E. LEE'S FORCES AT ANTIETAM CREEK IN MARYLAND.

THREE MONTHS LATER, ON JANUARY 1ST, 1863, LINCOLN SIGNED THE EMANCIPATION PROCLAMATION.

I NEVER IN MY LIFE FELT MORE CERTAIN THAT I WAS DOING RIGHT THAN I DO IN SIGNING THIS PAPER.

BESIDES ATTENDING TO THE WAR, LINCOLN SAW CROWDS OF PEOPLE WHO GATHERED OUTSIDE HIS OFFICE EVERY DAY TO ASK HIM FAVOURS. HIS SECRETARIES OBJECTED.

YOU SPEND ABOUT THREE-QUARTERS OF YOUR TIME JUST SEEING PEOPLE.

THEY DO NOT WANT VERY MUCH AND I HELP THEM VERY LITTLE. THE LEAST I CAN DO IS LISTEN TO THEM.

ONE DAY, A YOUNG SOLDIER ASKED FOR A CAPTAIN'S COMMISSION. LINCOLN ASKED HIM HIS AGE.

I'M SIXTEEN, SIR.

YOU ARE JUST A BOY. YOU ARE TOO YOUNG.

BUT I WAS TOLD THAT YOU COULD GIVE ANYONE A COMMISSION.

SO I COULD. BUT I ADVISE YOU TO DO YOUR DUTY AND PROMOTION WILL SEEK YOU. GO BACK TO THE ARMY LITTLE MAN AND BE THE BRAVE SOLDIER THAT YOU ARE.

NO MATTER HOW MANY PEOPLE HE SAW, LINCOLN NEVER LOST HIS SENSE OF HUMOUR.

I PRESUME, MR PRESIDENT, THAT YOU HAVE FORGOTTEN ME.

NO. YOUR NAME IS FLOOD. I SAW YOU LAST SOME TWELVE YEARS AGO. I AM GLAD TO SEE THAT THE FLOOD FLOWS ON.

HE ALSO FOUND TIME TO WRITE TO PEOPLE WHO HAD LOST RELATIVES IN THE WAR. HE HEARD THAT A WOMAN, MRS BIXBY, HAD LOST FIVE SONS.

I pray that our Heavenly Father may assuage the anguish of your bereavement, and leave you only the cherished memory of the loved and lost, and the solemn pride that must be yours to have laid so costly a sacrifice upon the altar of freedom.

Yours very sincerely and respectfully
A. Lincoln

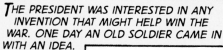

THE PRESIDENT WAS INTERESTED IN ANY INVENTION THAT MIGHT HELP WIN THE WAR. ONE DAY AN OLD SOLDIER CAME IN WITH AN IDEA.

MR PRESIDENT, I'VE MADE UP A COAT OF MAIL THAT EVERY MAN IN THE ARMY SHOULD HAVE. IT'S ABSOLUTELY BULLETPROOF.

IF THAT'S TRUE, THE ARMY SHALL HAVE IT. BUT WE MUST TEST IT FIRST. AS ITS INVENTOR, YOU CAN PUT IT ON AND WE'LL HAVE SOME SHARPSHOOTERS PRACTICE SHOOTING AT YOU.

THIS TEST WAS POSTPONED, BUT ANOTHER TOOK PLACE IN LINCOLN'S OFFICE.

NOW I'LL LIGHT THIS TORPEDO AND YOU'LL SEE HOW IT WORKS.

I RECKON I'LL GET OUT OF THE WAY IN CASE IT EXPLODES ON US.

MR LINCOLN, YOU MAKE A BETTER PRESIDENT THAN YOU WOULD A SOLDIER.

LINCOLN LIKED THE TORPEDO AND TOLD ITS INVENTORS TO KEEP WORKING ON IT. HE ALSO LIKED CHRISTOPHER SPENCER'S NEW BREECH-LOADING RIFLE.

WILL YOU TAKE IT APART, MR SPENCER, SO I CAN SEE THE INWARDNESS OF THE THING?

THE NEXT DAY, THEY TRIED THE RIFLE ON A TARGET. BEFORE HE AIMED, LINCOLN NOTICED THAT HIS COAT POCKET WAS TORN.

THIS DOESN'T LOOK QUITE RIGHT AND PROPER FOR THE CHIEF MAGISTRATE OF THE MIGHTY REPUBLIC.

THEN HE TRIED OUT THE RIFLE.

THIS GUN IS A WONDER!

ONCE A WEEK, EXCEPT IN SUMMER, LINCOLN AND HIS WIFE HELD AN EVENING RECEPTION. HE ONCE WELCOMED THE FAMOUS DWARFS, MR AND MRS TOM THUMB.

TONIGHT YOU BOTH ARE THE CENTRE OF ATTRACTION. YOU HAVE THROWN ME COMPLETELY IN THE SHADE.

PEOPLE THOUGHT THESE RECEPTIONS MUST BE A BURDEN FOR THE WORRIED PRESIDENT.

DOESN'T SHAKING HANDS CONSTANTLY WEAR YOU OUT?

THE PULL ON MY HAND IS EASIER TO ENDURE THAN THE PULL ON MY HEART WHEN PEOPLE ASK ME FOR FAVOURS THAT I HAVE NO POWER TO GRANT.

AT NIGHT, LINCOLN USUALLY WENT TO THE WAR DEPARTMENT TO HEAR THE LATEST NEWS OF THE WAR.

GOOD NEWS TONIGHT, MR PRESIDENT. THERE'S NO NEWS.

THAT'S NOT AN ESPECIALLY GOOD REASON, MY YOUNG FRIEND. A FISHERMAN DOESN'T THINK HE'S LUCKY IF HE DOESN'T GET A BITE.

HE OFTEN READ BEFORE HE WENT TO BED.

YOU BOYS STOP YOUR LABOURS AND LET ME READ YOU THIS HUMDINGER OF A FUNNY STORY.

HE RELAXED WITH MUSIC OR THE THEATRE. ONCE, WHILE A FIERCE BATTLE WAS ON, HE WENT TO THE OPERA.

I SUPPOSE PEOPLE MAY THINK IT HARDHEARTED OF ME TO TAKE AMUSEMENT AT SUCH A TIME. BUT THE TRUTH IS THAT I MUST HAVE A CHANGE OF SOME SORT OR DIE.

LINCOLN WAS HEARTSICK AT THE SLOW PROGRESS OF THE WAR. IN JANUARY, 1863, HE PUT GENERAL JOSEPH HOOKER IN COMMAND OF THE ARMY OF THE POTOMAC.

HOW WOULD YOU LIKE TO COME WITH ME TO VISIT FIGHTING JOE HOOKER, TAD?

OH, PA, THAT WOULD BE GREAT! AND MAYBE I COULD RIDE WITH THE TROOPS!

LINCOLN REVIEWED HOOKER'S ARMY.

IN MAY, THE CONFEDERATE ARMY TOOK HOOKER BY SURPRISE AT CHANCELLORSVILLE, VIRGINIA. HOOKER ORDERED A RETREAT.

LINCOLN RELIEVED HOOKER OF HIS COMMAND. IN HIS PLACE HE PUT GENERAL GEORGE MEADE WITH ORDERS TO STOP THE CONFEDERATE ARMY, WHICH WAS STEADILY MOVING NORTH. IN JULY, MEADE BEAT THE CONFEDERATES UNDER ROBERT E. LEE AT GETTYSBURG, PENNSYLVANIA. IT WAS THE TURNING POINT OF THE WAR.

BUT LINCOLN WAS UPSET TO HEAR THAT MEADE HAD NOT FOLLOWED LEE AND CRUSHED HIM DECISIVELY.

MEADE TELLS ME HE HAS DRIVEN LEE FROM OUR SOIL! BUT HE LET HIM GET AWAY! I TELL YOU, WE NEED A GENERAL WHO WILL REALISE THAT THE WHOLE COUNTRY IS OUR SOIL!

A FEW DAYS LATER, WORD CAME THAT GENERAL ULYSSES S. GRANT HAD TAKEN THE CITY OF VICKSBURG, MISSISSIPPI.

I SAID THAT IF GRANT TOOK VICKSBURG, THEN HE WOULD BE MY MAN AND I HIS FOR THE REST OF THE WAR. AND SO IT WILL BE!

EARLY IN 1864 GRANT WAS GIVEN COMMAND OF THE UNION ARMIES. IN MARCH HE MET LINCOLN FOR THE FIRST TIME.

YOU ARE THE GENERAL I HAVE BEEN LOOKING FOR. YOU NEVER GIVE UP!

THAT SPRING, GRANT BEGAN A CAMPAIGN AGAINST THE CONFEDERATE ARMY. THERE WERE WEEKS OF DESPERATE FIGHTING IN VIRGINIA.

THE UNION TROOPS WERE VICTORIOUS, BUT THE NUMBER OF DEAD AND WOUNDED WAS HIGH.

LOOK YONDER AT THOSE POOR FELLOWS BACK FROM VIRGINIA. THIS SUFFERING, THIS LOSS OF LIFE, IS DREADFUL.

IN JULY, WASHINGTON WAS THREATENED BY AN APPROACHING CONFEDERATE ARMY. LINCOLN WATCHED UNION TROOPS MARCH OUT TO DEFEAT THEM. HE WAS HEEDLESS OF HIS OWN SAFETY.

GET DOWN, YOU FOOL, BEFORE YOU GET SHOT!

ALTHOUGH THE CIVIL WAR CONTINUED, PRESIDENTIAL ELECTIONS WERE HELD. ON THE MORNING OF ELECTION DAY, 1864, LINCOLN AND TAD WATCHED THE SOLDERS VOTE.

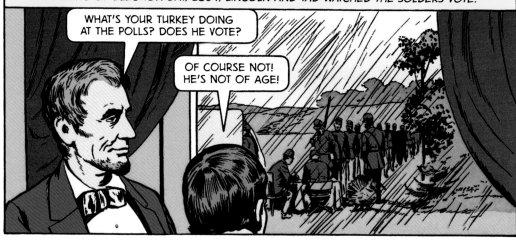

WHAT'S YOUR TURKEY DOING AT THE POLLS? DOES HE VOTE?

OF COURSE NOT! HE'S NOT OF AGE!

IN THE EVENING LINCOLN WENT TO THE WAR DEPARTMENT TO HEAR THE ELECTION RETURNS.

ISN'T IT GREAT THAT OUR OLD ENEMY, DAVIS, IS BEING DEFEATED IN MARYLAND?

I GUESS YOU HAVE MORE OF A FEELING OF PERSONAL RESENTMENT THAN I. PERHAPS I HAVE TOO LITTLE OF IT, BUT I NEVER THOUGHT IT PAID. A MAN HAS NO TIME TO SPEND HALF HIS LIFE IN QUARRELS.

WHEN LINCOLN'S VICTORY WAS ALMOST CERTAIN, HE HAD A MIDNIGHT SUPPER.

I AM REMINDED OF HOW I WENT HOME EXHAUSTED AFTER THE ELECTION IN 1860. I LAY DOWN ON A SOFA. AS I GAZED INTO A MIRROR OPPOSITE ME, I SAW TWO DISTINCT IMAGES OF MY FACE.

"ONE IMAGE WAS PALER THAN THE OTHER. I COULD ONLY CONCLUDE THAT IT MEANT I WOULD BE ELECTED FOR TWO TERMS BUT THAT I WOULD NOT LIVE THROUGH THE SECOND ONE."

DREAM OR NO DREAM, YOU ARE IN CONSTANT DANGER. I WISH YOU WOULD BE MORE CAREFUL ABOUT GOING OUT ALONE AND UNGUARDED.

IF ANYONE REALLY WISHES TO KILL ME, HILL, NO AMOUNT OF CARE WILL PROTECT ME. BESIDES, I FEEL IT ESSENTIAL THAT THE PEOPLE KNOW I COME AMONG THEM WITHOUT FEAR.

GRANT AND HIS GENERALS WERE STEADILY BRINGING THE WAR TO A CLOSE. IN DECEMBER GENERAL WILLIAM TECUMSEH SHERMAN MARCHED VICTORIOUSLY THROUGH GEORGIA.

THROUGHOUT THE WINTER GRANT BESIEGED PETERSBURG, VIRGINIA, WHICH WAS THE GATEWAY TO THE CAPITAL OF THE CONFEDERACY – RICHMOND. IN MARCH, 1865, HE INVITED LINCOLN TO LOOK OVER THE BATTLEFIELD.

ARE WE REALLY GOING TO SEE GENERAL GRANT, PA?

YES, TADDIE. WE MAY EVEN SEE RICHMOND, IF WE'RE LUCKY.

LINCOLN MET WITH GRANT, SHERMAN AND ADMIRAL DAVID PORTER.

HOW ARE WE TO TREAT THE SOUTH AND ITS ARMIES AT THE WAR'S END, MR PRESIDENT?

AS MERCIFULLY AND KINDLY AS POSSIBLE, GENERAL. THE FASTER THE SOUTH AND ITS PEOPLE ARE ACCEPTED AS UNITED STATES CITIZENS, THE SOONER WE WILL BE ONE NATION AGAIN.

FOUR DAYS LATER A WAR CORRESPONDENT ARRIVED FROM GRANT'S HEADQUARTERS WITH SOME CAPTURED CONFEDERATE FLAGS.

HERE IS SOMETHING MATERIAL, SOMETHING I CAN SEE, FEEL AND UNDERSTAND. THESE MEAN VICTORY. THESE ARE VICTORY.

ON APRIL 2ND THE UNION FORCES ATTACKED PETERSBURG, AND THE CONFEDERATE FORCES WITHDREW. LINCOLN JOINED GRANT IN THE FALLEN CITY.

PETERSBURG IS OURS, MR PRESIDENT. RICHMOND WILL FALL ANY MINUTE.

THE END IS NEAR, GENERAL. THANK YOU.

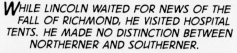

WHILE LINCOLN WAITED FOR NEWS OF THE FALL OF RICHMOND, HE VISITED HOSPITAL TENTS. HE MADE NO DISTINCTION BETWEEN NORTHERNER AND SOUTHERNER.

MR PRESIDENT, YOU DO NOT WANT TO GO IN THERE. THEY ARE REBEL PRISONERS.

THEN THAT IS JUST WHERE I DO WANT TO GO.

MR PRESIDENT, DO YOU KNOW THAT YOU OFFER YOUR HAND TO A CONFEDERATE COLONEL WHO HAS FOUGHT YOU AS HARD AS HE COULD FOR FOUR YEARS?

WELL, I HOPE A CONFEDERATE COLONEL WILL NOT REFUSE ME HIS HAND.

NO, SIR, I WILL NOT.

LINCOLN TRIED TO VISIT EVERY ONE OF THE THOUSANDS OF WOUNDED MEN. AT THE DAY'S END, HIS ARM WAS ALMOST LAME.

YOUR RIGHT ARM MUST HURT FROM ALL THE HAND SHAKING YOU'VE BEEN DOING.

IT'S NOT SO BAD, DOCTOR. I'VE GOT STRONG MUSCLES LEFT OVER FROM MY YOUTH. LET'S SEE WHAT I CAN DO WITH THIS AXE NOW.

AND HE SPLIT A LOG AS EASILY AS A YOUNG MAN COULD.

ON APRIL 3RD NEWS CAME THAT RICHMOND HAD FALLEN THE PREVIOUS DAY. ON APRIL 4TH LINCOLN SAILED UP THE RIVER TO THE CAPITAL OF THE CONFEDERACY. HE WAS MET ON THE SHORE BY A GROUP OF NEGROES.

GLORY HALLELUJAH! HERE'S OUR GREAT MESSIAH!

DON'T KNEEL TO ME. YOU MUST KNEEL ONLY TO GOD AND THANK HIM FOR YOUR FREEDOM.

HE WALKED FEARLESSLY THROUGH THE SILENT STREETS.

KEEP YOUR EYES SHARP FOR GUNS, SIR. THIS IS NOT THE SAFEST SPOT FOR THE PRESIDENT OF THE UNITED STATES TO BE IN TODAY.

THEY WENT TO THE FORMER EXECUTIVE MANSION OF THE CONFEDERACY.

SO THIS IS THE CHAIR IN WHICH JEFFERSON DAVIS SAT AS PRESIDENT OF THE CONFEDERATE STATES OF AMERICA. WELL, IT WILL SOON ALL BE THE UNITED STATES AGAIN.

LINCOLN TALKED TO THE NORTHERN GENERAL WHO OCCUPIED RICHMOND.

HOW SHALL I DEAL WITH THE PEOPLE OF RICHMOND, MR PRESIDENT?

IF I WERE IN YOUR PLACE, I'D LET 'EM UP EASY, LET 'EM UP EASY.

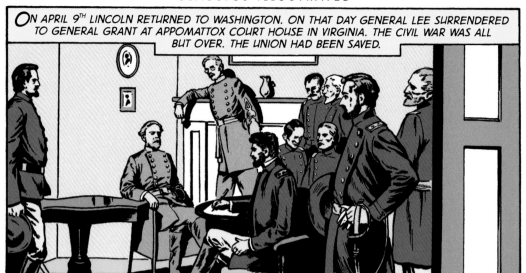

ON APRIL 9TH LINCOLN RETURNED TO WASHINGTON. ON THAT DAY GENERAL LEE SURRENDERED TO GENERAL GRANT AT APPOMATTOX COURT HOUSE IN VIRGINIA. THE CIVIL WAR WAS ALL BUT OVER. THE UNION HAD BEEN SAVED.

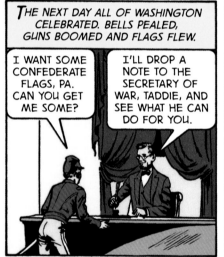

THE NEXT DAY ALL OF WASHINGTON CELEBRATED. BELLS PEALED, GUNS BOOMED AND FLAGS FLEW.

I WANT SOME CONFEDERATE FLAGS, PA. CAN YOU GET ME SOME?

I'LL DROP A NOTE TO THE SECRETARY OF WAR, TADDIE, AND SEE WHAT HE CAN DO FOR YOU.

A CROWD GATHERED AT THE WHITE HOUSE.

LINCOLN! LINCOLN!

LINCOLN CAME OUT FOR A FEW MINUTES.

I THINK IT'S TIME WE HEARD THE REBEL SONG "DIXIE" HERE IN THE NORTH. LET'S HAVE A ROUND OF IT.

THE NEXT NIGHT LINCOLN MADE A FORMAL SPEECH IN HONOUR OF LEE'S SURRENDER. IN THE CROWD WAS AN ACTOR, JOHN WILKES BOOTH, A FANATIC SOUTHERNER.

THAT'S THE LAST SPEECH HE WILL EVER MAKE.

LINCOLN SPENT THE NEXT FEW DAYS ARRANGING FOR A PEACEFUL END TO THE WAR. ON FRIDAY, APRIL 14TH, HIS SON, CAPTAIN ROBERT LINCOLN, WAS AT HOME WITH HIS FAMILY.

I THOUGHT YOU MIGHT BE AMUSED TO HAVE A PICTURE OF GENERAL LEE, FATHER.

NOT REALLY AMUSED, BOB. HE HAS A GOOD FACE. AND I AM GLAD THE WAR IS OVER.

REMEMBER, MY DEAR, WE HAVE TICKETS TO FORD'S THEATRE TONIGHT.

I'LL REMEMBER, THOUGH I DON'T MUCH FEEL LIKE GOING, BUT PEOPLE WILL BE EXPECTING ME.

THAT MORNING LINCOLN MET WITH HIS CABINET AND OTHER OFFICIALS. THEY DISCUSSED WHAT TO DO WITH SOUTHERN LEADERS.

I HOPE THERE WILL BE NO PERSECUTION. NO ONE NEED EXPECT ME TO TAKE ANY PART IN HANGING OR KILLING THESE MEN. ENOUGH LIVES HAVE BEEN SACRIFICED.

LINCOLN WORKED AND SAW CALLERS UNTIL LATE IN THE AFTERNOON. THEN...

WON'T YOU JOIN ME FOR A DRIVE?

I'D BE DELIGHTED, MY DEAR. YOU KNOW, I'VE ACCOMPLISHED A LOT TODAY TOWARD FINISHING UP THE WAR PEACEABLY.

WOULD YOU LIKE SOMEONE TO COME WITH US?

NO, I AM SO CONTENT THAT I PREFER TO RIDE BY OURSELVES TODAY. WE CAN TALK ABOUT THE HAPPY DAYS AHEAD OF US.

IN THE EVENING THE LINCOLNS AND TWO GUESTS WENT TO THE THEATRE.

AT NINE O'CLOCK THE PRESIDENT'S BODYGUARD LEFT.

IT'S NO FUN SITTING IN THERE. LET'S HAVE A DRINK.

SHORTLY AFTER TEN O'CLOCK JOHN WILKES BOOTH ENTERED.

YOU DON'T WANT A TICKET FROM ME, DO YOU?

OF COURSE NOT, MR BOOTH. YOU CAN COME IN ON THE HOUSE.

UPSTAIRS, LINCOLN WAS ENJOYING THE PLAY.

THIS IS WONDERFUL! I'M GLAD WE CAME.

BOOTH WENT TO THE PRESIDENT'S BOX.

NOW'S MY CHANCE! EVERYONE'S LAUGHING AND LOOKING AT THE STAGE!

HE OPENED THE DOOR, WENT IN AND SHOT ABRAHAM LINCOLN.

THEN HE LEAPED FROM THE BOX TO THE STAGE. ONE LEG CAUGHT IN A FLAG AND BROKE AS HE LANDED, BUT HE ESCAPED.

REVENGE FOR THE SOUTH!

FOR GOD'S SAKE, WHAT IS IT? WHAT HAS HAPPENED?

THAT MAN HAS SHOT THE PRESIDENT!

A DOCTOR IN THE AUDIENCE EXAMINED LINCOLN.

HIS WOUND IS MORTAL. IT IS IMPOSSIBLE FOR HIM TO RECOVER.

LINCOLN WAS CARRIED TO A HOUSE ACROSS THE STREET FROM THE THEATRE.

GO AND FETCH HIS SON, ROBERT, AND HIS DOCTOR AND PASTOR.

ALL THROUGH THE NIGHT, THERE WAS A LONG WAIT BY HIS BEDSIDE.

AT 7:22 THE NEXT MORNING, HE DIED.

NOW HE BELONGS TO THE AGES.

FOR NEARLY TWO WEEKS JOHN WILKES BOOTH WAS PURSUED RELENTLESSLY. HE WAS CORNERED IN A BARN IN VIRGINIA ON APRIL 26TH.

LINCOLN'S BODY WAS CARRIED TO SPRINGFIELD IN A FUNERAL TRAIN. NORTHERNERS WEPT FOR THE MAN WHOSE FAITH IN THE UNION BROUGHT THE NATION THROUGH ITS DARKEST HOUR. SOUTHERNERS MOURNED THE GENEROUS FOE WHO FORGAVE THEM AND WELCOMED THEM BACK TO THE UNION.

AT HIS GRAVE IN SPRINGFIELD, ILLINOIS, HIS SECOND INAUGURAL ADDRESS WAS READ.

"WITH MALICE TOWARD NONE; WITH CHARITY FOR ALL; WITH FIRMNESS IN THE RIGHT, AS GOD GIVES US TO SEE THE RIGHT, LET US STRIVE ON TO FINISH THE WORK WE ARE IN; TO BIND UP THE NATION'S WOUNDS; TO CARE FOR HIM WHO SHALL HAVE BORNE THE BATTLE, AND FOR HIS WIDOW AND HIS ORPHAN – TO DO ALL WHICH MAY ACHIEVE AND CHERISH A JUST AND A LASTING PEACE, AMONG OURSELVES, AND WITH ALL NATIONS."

THE END

Conspiracy

The assassination of President Abraham Lincoln was a carefully planned conspiracy. Lincoln was not the only man marked for death that day. The Vice President, Andrew Johnson, and the Secretary of State, William H. Seward, were also included in the assassination plans. The attack on Johnson was not carried out because the assigned murderer lost his nerve. Secretary Seward, however, was not so fortunate.

While John Wilkes Booth was in Ford's Theatre about to murder Lincoln, two of his comrades, Lewis Powell (also known as Lewis Payne, or Paine) and David Herold, approached the home of Secretary Seward. While Herold waited outside, Powell walked up to the front door and knocked loudly. The door was opened by a young servant. Paine told the servant that he had medicine for Secretary Seward, who had been badly injured in an accident and was confined to bed with a concussion of the brain, a broken arm and other injuries. Powell insisted that he had to deliver the medicine to Seward personally. The servant let him in.

On the top floor of the house, Secretary Seward's son, Frederick, the Assistant Secretary of State, heard the noise downstairs. He put on his dressing gown and went into the hall. There he saw Lewis Powell coming towards him. Frederick Seward demanded to know what the commotion was about. Powell said he had some medicine for the Secretary of State.

Frederick Seward said that he would see that it was delivered. Powell shook his head and indicated that it had to be delivered by him personally to Secretary Seward.

Powell waited while Frederick Seward went up to the front of the hall to a door on the left side. This told Powell where Secretary Seward's room was. When Frederick Seward returned, he told Powell that it was impossible for him to see his father as he was asleep and couldn't be disturbed. Powell hesitated, then pulled out a pistol and fired at young Seward. The hammer of the pistol clicked but no sound was heard. Powell then hit Frederick Seward several times on the head with the butt of the gun. Frederick Seward fell and Powell hit him several more times.

Outside, Powell's accomplice heard the commotion and ran off.

Meanwhile, in the house, Powell saw that his pistol was broken. He threw it at Frederick Seward and drew a knife. Then he hurried to Secretary Seward's bedroom. He pushed against the door and discovered that someone was leaning against it.

Powell crashed his weight against the door and stumbled inside. The room was in total darkness except for a tiny glimmer of light from the hall. The assassin saw a moving figure and slashed at it. A man screamed out in pain. Then Powell jumped on the bed, and when he felt the helpless figure of Secretary Seward, he struck with his knife. Suddenly someone grabbed Powell's arm. As he turned, he found himself fighting with two people. They struggled to pull him off the bed. Meanwhile, Secretary Seward rolled off the bed onto the floor to protect himself.

Powell managed to escape his would-be captors. He ran into the hall. There he saw another man coming towards him. It was a State Department messenger. When he came close, Powell raised his knife and plunged it into the messenger's chest. Then Powell ran downstairs and into the street.

The Seward home was a terrible sight. The messenger was badly wounded. Frederick Seward was in a coma. A male nurse was also badly wounded. Major Augustus Seward, another of Secretary Seward's sons, was injured. Fanny Seward, Secretary Seward's daughter, who had been battered about when Powell entered the bedroom, was unconscious.

Secretary Seward eventually recovered, as did others who were in the Seward home that night.

Lewis Powell and David Herold were caught, tried, convicted and hanged.

Lewis Powell   David Herold

Soldier, Lawyer and Justice

In July, 1864, toward the close of the Civil War, a Confederate army threatened Washington, D.C. At Fort Stevens President Abraham Lincoln watched the Union forces go out to battle the Southerners. Heedless of his safety, his long, lanky figure and high hat presented a fine target for the enemy.

Suddenly a young Union captain in the fort shouted, "Get down, you fool, before you get shot." President Lincoln stepped back. "I am glad you know how to talk to a civilian," he said.

The captain who spoke so roughly to the President of the United States was twenty-three-year-old Oliver Wendell Holmes Jr., who later became a learned and respected justice of the Supreme Court.

Holmes fought in many battles during the Civil War. Among them was the battle of Antietam. At this battle, Captain Holmes's company was ordered forward. Holmes got them through a wood and out to a cornfield, but the morning was exceptionally misty and Holmes completely lost his bearings.

Suddenly there was a cry as the enemy was sighted in the rear. Men fell wounded and dead as all about them other men rushed to the attack. Through all this the company did not break rank. Eventually the soldiers left the battle scene, but not Captain Holmes. He lay on the ground, shot through the neck.

The first thing that Holmes was fully conscious of after he had been wounded was someone on each side of him, holding him up. He was weak and losing blood, and as he struggled to take a step, he stumbled. The bullet had gone sideways through his neck, and fortunately had missed his windpipe. But the pain was bad and getting worse. His collar stuck fast to his skin so that he couldn't turn his head. He was taken to a farmhouse, which was filled with other wounded men.

Holmes was sent home to recover. After six weeks, his wound healed and he returned to battle. At Chancellorsville, fifteen miles from Fredericksburg, he was wounded again. This wound troubled him for many years. It was caused by shrapnel that caught the heel of his foot, tearing through ligaments and tendons. It was Holmes's third wound, for even before Antietam, he had been wounded at Ball's Bluff.

After the Civil War, Holmes, a Harvard University graduate, was admitted to the bar to practice law. After some private practice, he taught law at Harvard. In 1881, he wrote *The Common Law*, which is considered one of the classic books on law.

In 1882, Holmes was appointed a justice of the Supreme Court of Massachusetts. In 1902, he was made a justice of the Supreme Court of the United States. As a Supreme Court justice, he became known as "The Great Dissenter." Many times when the Supreme Court handed down a decision, Justice Holmes delivered a minority opinion or dissent. His dissents were so powerful and sound that they influenced public thought and later many became a part of the law.

Holmes served as a Supreme Court justice until he was ninety-one years old, resigning in 1932. In 1933, President Franklin D. Roosevelt visited him and found him reading the Greek philosopher, Plato. "To improve my mind, Mr President," explained Holmes.

Holmes died in March, 1935. At his funeral, eight infantrymen fired a volley for each wound inflicted upon him during the Civil War: Ball's Bluff, Antietam and Fredericksburg.

Supreme Court Justice Oliver Wendell Holmes Jr.